SUPER EASY SONGBOOK

HARRY STYLES

T0071606

ISBN 978-1-70517-458-6

Visit Hal Leonard Online at
www.halleonard.com

World headquarters, contact:
Hal Leonard
7777 West Bluemound Road
Milwaukee, WI 53213
Email: info@halleonard.com

In Europe, contact:
Hal Leonard Europe Limited
1 Red Place
London, W1K 6PL
Email: info@halleonardeurope.com

In Australia, contact:
Hal Leonard Australia Pty. Ltd.
4 Lentara Court
Cheltenham, Victoria, 3192 Australia
Email: info@halleonard.com.au

Adore You

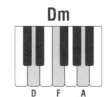 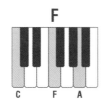 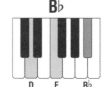 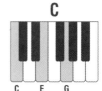

Words and Music by Harry Styles,
Thomas Hull, Tyler Johnson
and Amy Allen

Moderate Pop Rock

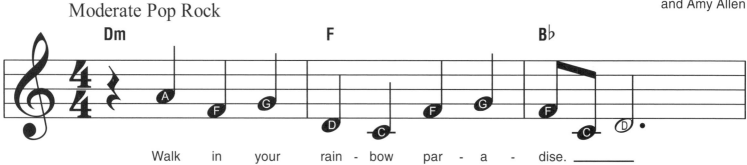

Walk in your rain-bow par-a-dise. _____

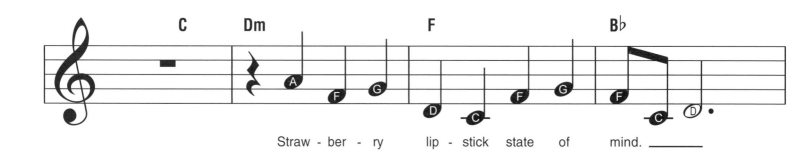

Straw-ber-ry lip-stick state of mind. _____

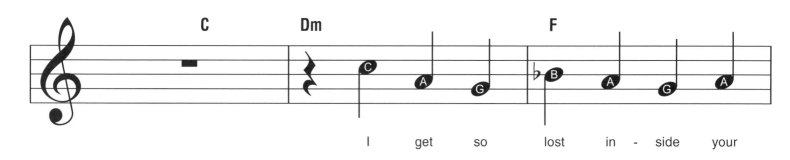

I get so lost in-side your

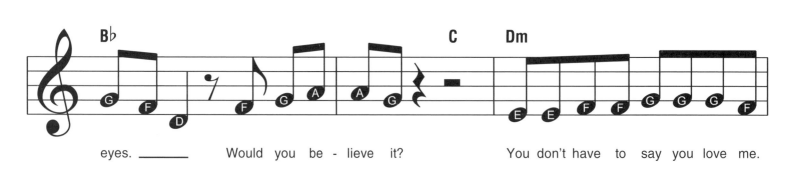

eyes. _____ Would you be-lieve it? You don't have to say you love me.

As It Was

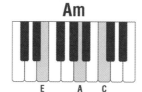
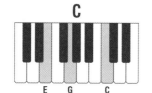
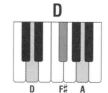
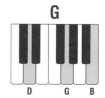

Words and Music by Harry Styles,
Thomas Hull and Tyler Johnson

With energy

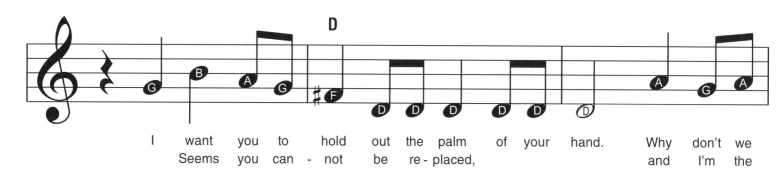

Hold - ing me back, _____ grav - i - ty's hold - ing me back. _____
Noth - ing to say _____ when ev - 'ry - thing gets in the way. _____

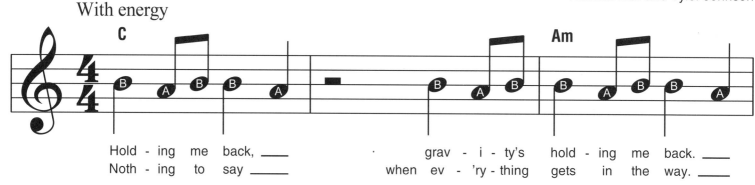

I want you to hold out the palm of your hand. Why don't we
Seems you can - not be re - placed, and I'm the

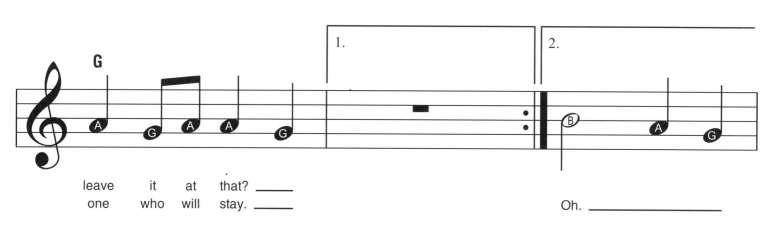

leave it at that? _____
one who will stay. _____

Oh. _____

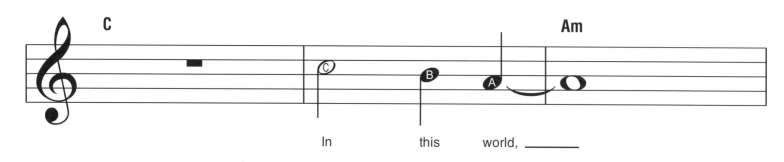

In this world, _____

it's just us. _____ You

know it's not the same as it was. In this world, ___

___ it's just us. _____ You

know it's not the same as it was,

as it was, as it was. _____

(Instrumental)

Boyfriends

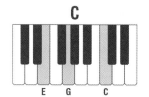
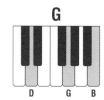
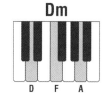
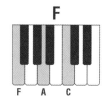
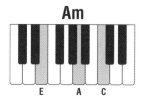

Words and Music by Harry Styles,
Thomas Hull, Tobias Jesso Jr.
and Tyler Johnson

Gentle Ballad

Boy - friends, _____ they think you're so

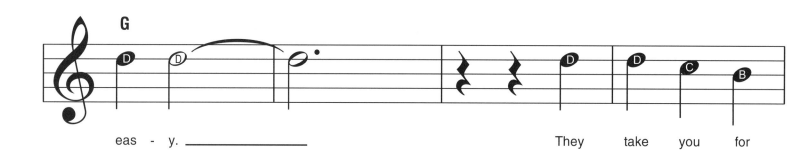

eas - y. _____ They take you for

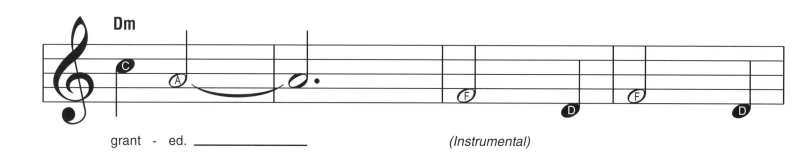

grant - ed. _____ (Instrumental)

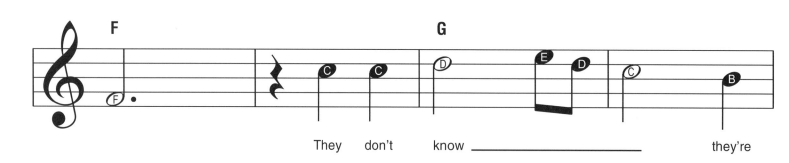

They don't know _____ they're

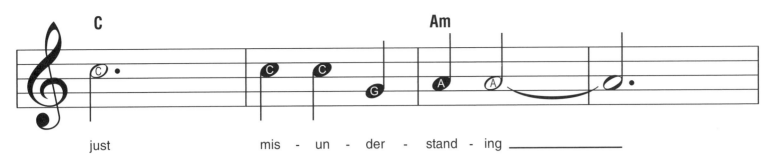

just   mis - un - der - stand - ing

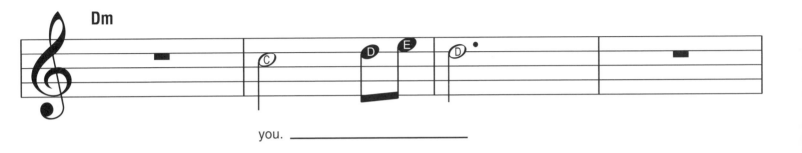

you.

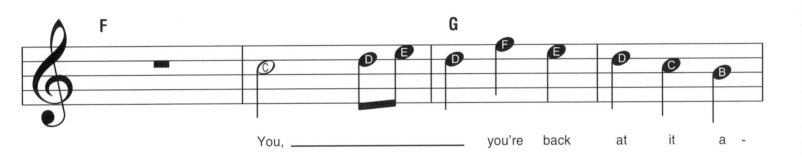

You,   you're   back   at   it   a -

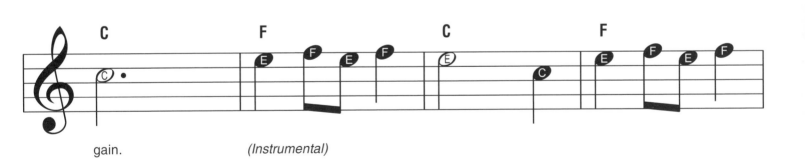

gain.   *(Instrumental)*

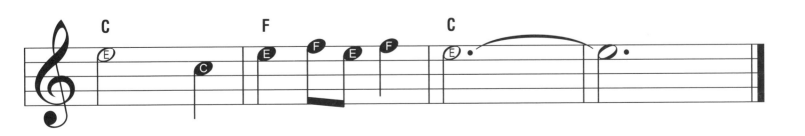

Carolina

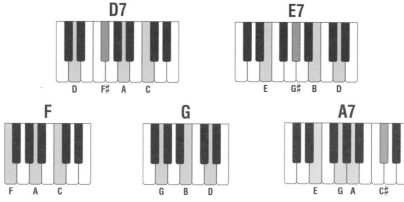

Words and Music by Harry Styles,
Thomas Hull, Jeff Bhasker, Tyler Johnson,
Alex Salibian, Mitch Rowland and Ryan Nasci

Moderate groove

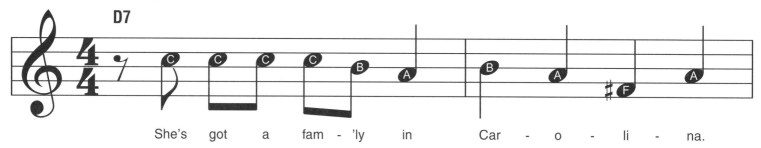

She's got a fam-'ly in Car-o-li-na.

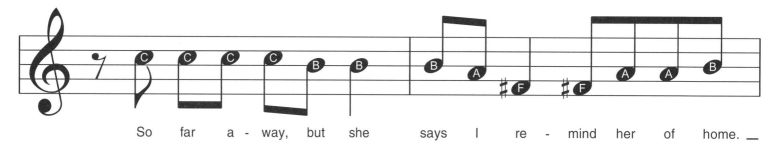

So far a-way, but she says I re-mind her of home.

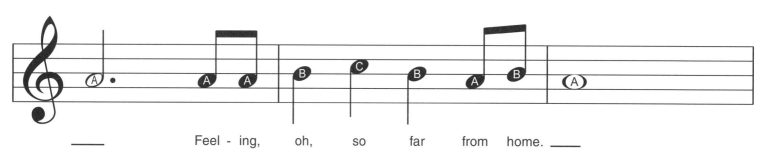

Feel-ing, oh, so far from home.

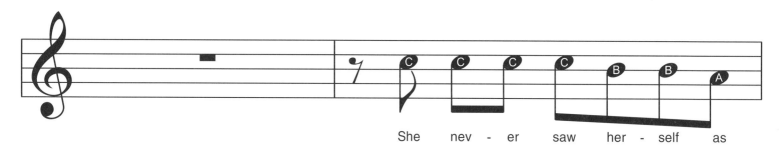

She nev-er saw her-self as

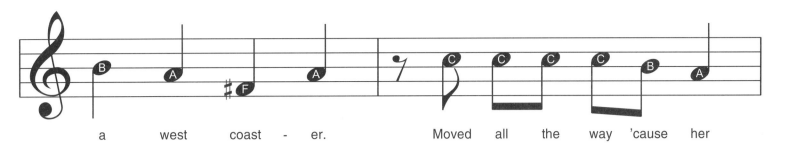

a west coast - er. Moved all the way 'cause her

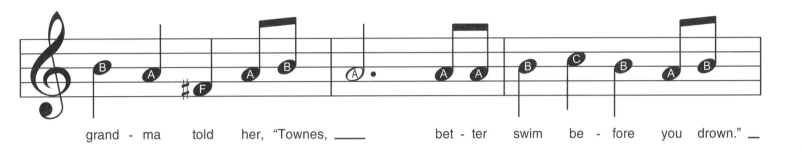

grand - ma told her, "Townes, _____ bet - ter swim be - fore you drown." _

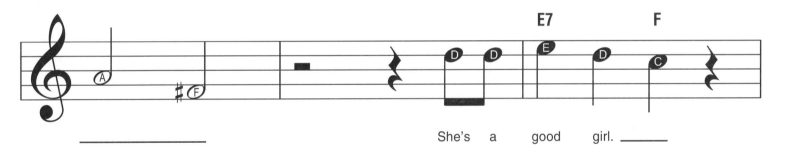

_____ She's a good girl. _____

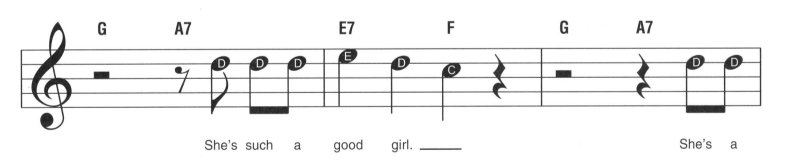

She's such a good girl. _____ She's a

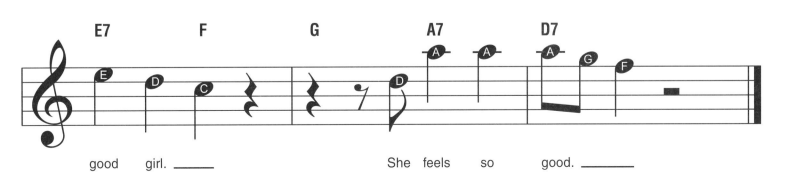

good girl. _____ She feels so good. _____

Falling

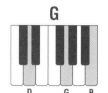 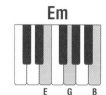 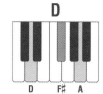 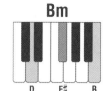 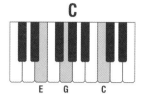

Words and Music by Harry Styles
and Thomas Hull

Moderate Ballad

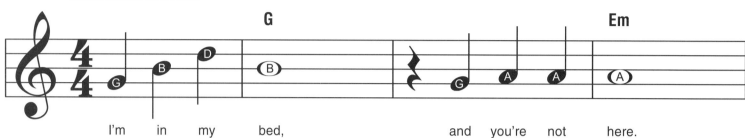

I'm in my bed, and you're not here.

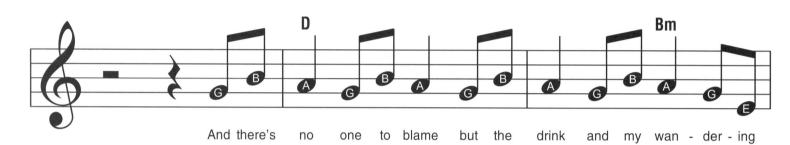

And there's no one to blame but the drink and my wan - der - ing

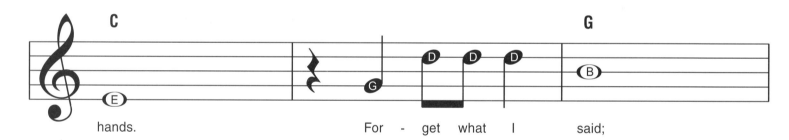

hands. For - get what I said;

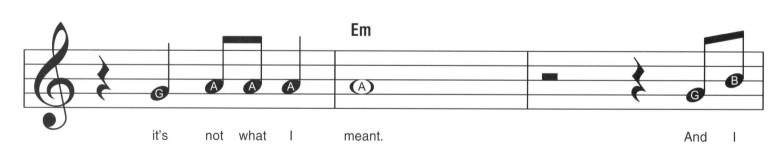

it's not what I meant. And I

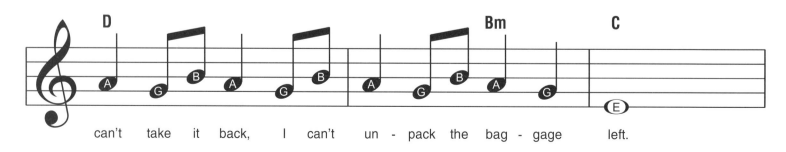

can't take it back, I can't un - pack the bag - gage left.

Golden

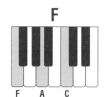
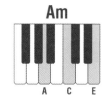
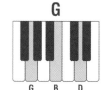
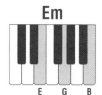

Words and Music by Harry Styles,
Thomas Hull, Mitchell Rowland
and Tyler Johnson

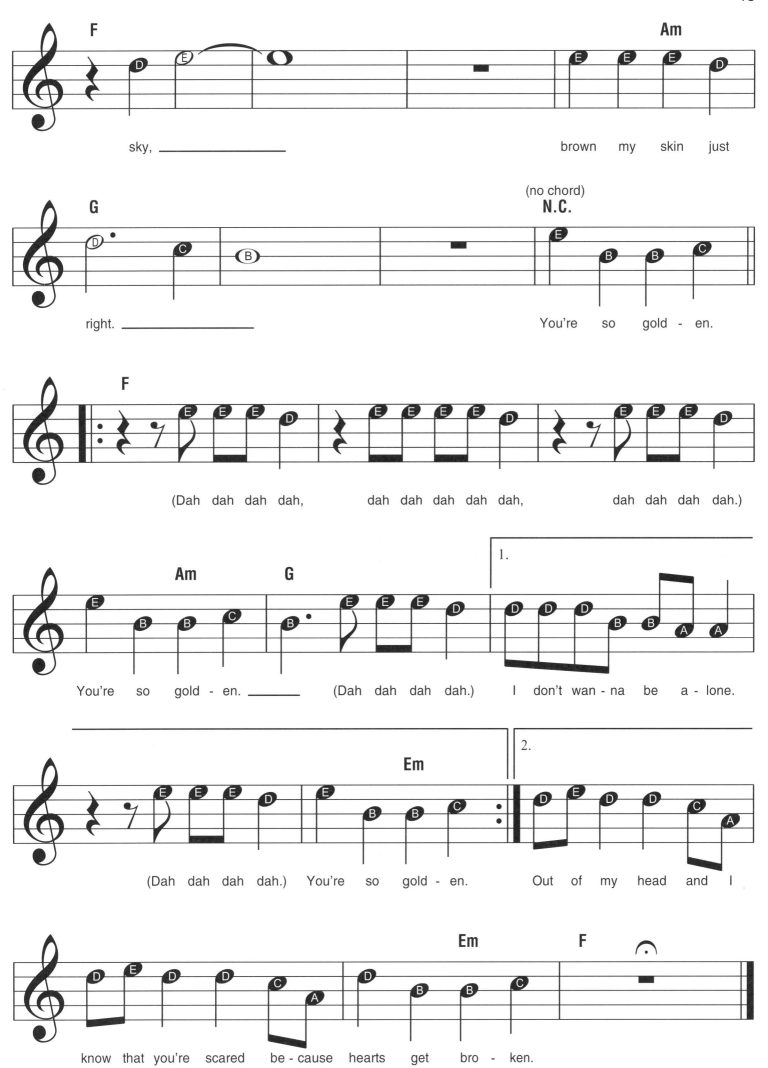

Kiwi

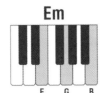 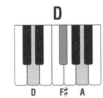 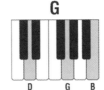 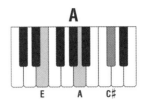

Words and Music by Harry Styles,
Jeff Bhasker, Tyler Johnson, Alex Salibian,
Mitch Rowland and Ryan Nasci

Driving Rock Shuffle

She worked her way through a cheap pack of cig - a - rettes. Hard

liq - uor mixed with a bit of in - tel - lect. And all the

boys, they were say - ing they were in - to it. Such a

pret - ty face on a pret - ty neck. She's driv - ing me

cra - zy, but I'm in - to it, but I'm in - to it, I'm kind of

Late Night Talking

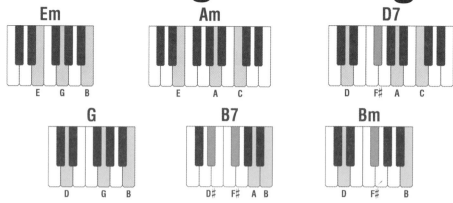

Words and Music by Harry Styles
and Thomas Hull

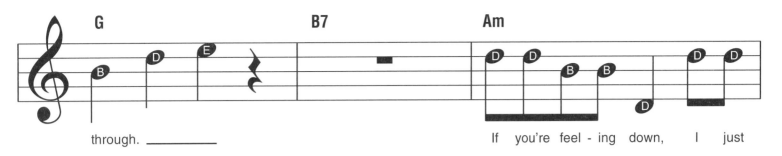

through. _____

If you're feel - ing down, I just

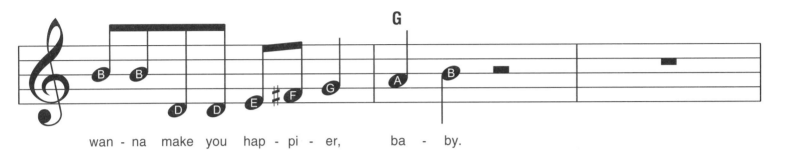

wan - na make you hap - pi - er, ba - by.

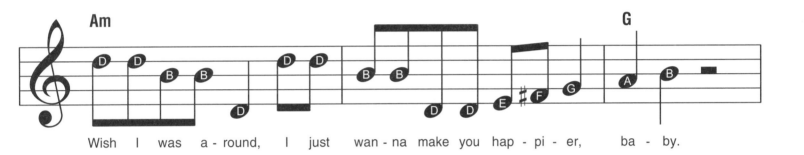

Wish I was a - round, I just wan - na make you hap - pi - er, ba - by.

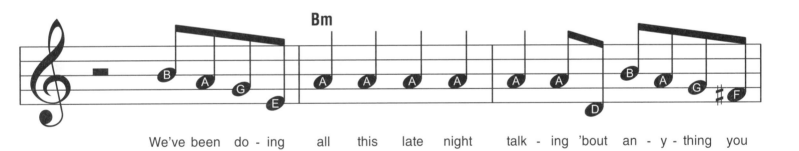

We've been do - ing all this late night talk - ing 'bout an - y - thing you

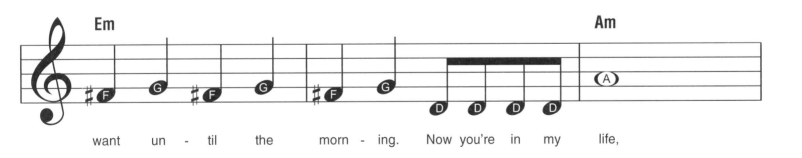

want un - til the morn - ing. Now you're in my life,

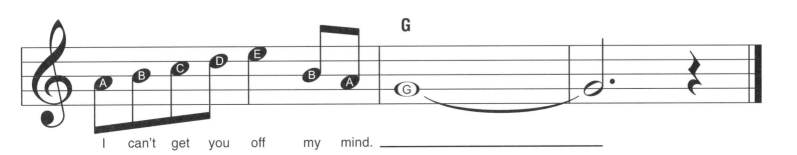

I can't get you off my mind. _____

Lights Up

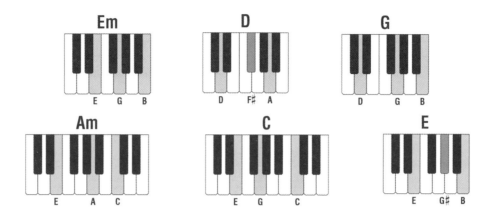

Words and Music by Harry Styles,
Thomas Hull and Tyler Johnson

Moderate groove

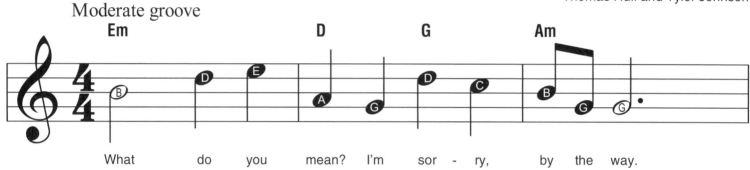

What do you mean? I'm sor - ry, by the way.

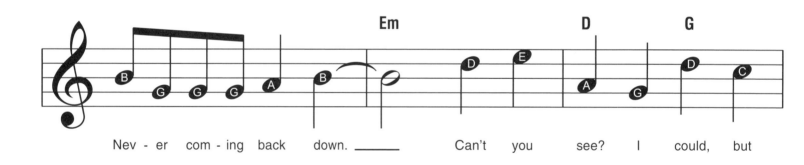

Nev - er com - ing back down. _____ Can't you see? I could, but

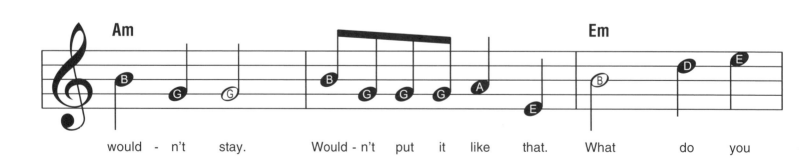

would - n't stay. Would - n't put it like that. What do you

mean? I'm sor - ry, by the way. Nev - er com - ing a - round. ___

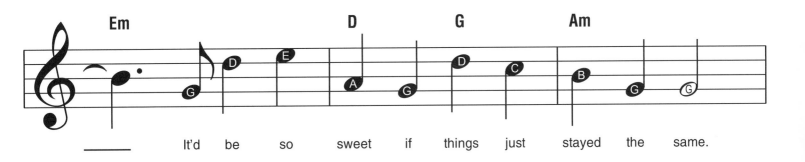

___ It'd be so sweet if things just stayed the same.

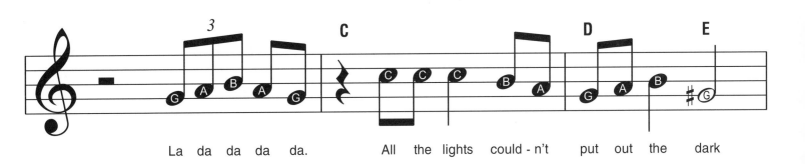

La da da da da. All the lights could - n't put out the dark

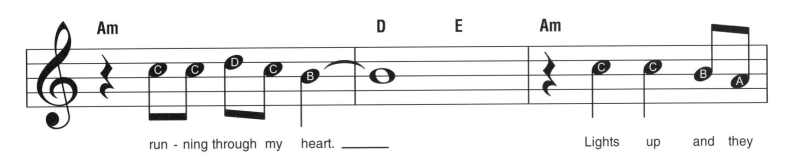

run - ning through my heart. ___ Lights up and they

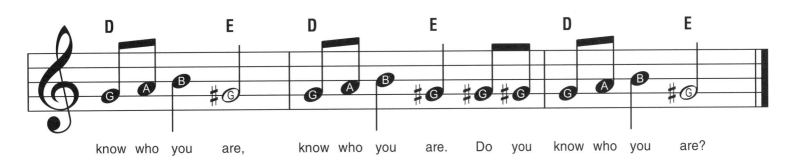

know who you are, know who you are. Do you know who you are?

Matilda

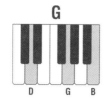
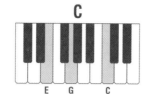

Words and Music by Harry Styles,
Thomas Hull, Tyler Johnson
and Amy Allen

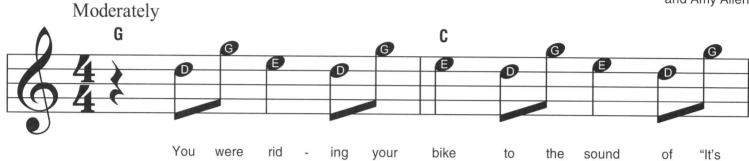

You were rid - ing your bike to the sound of "It's

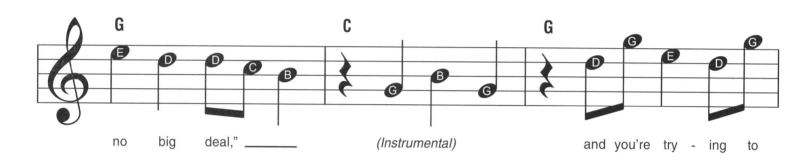

no big deal," _____ *(Instrumental)* and you're try - ing to

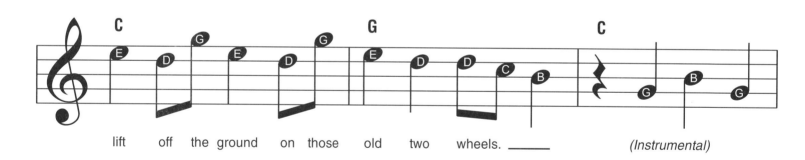

lift off the ground on those old two wheels. _____ *(Instrumental)*

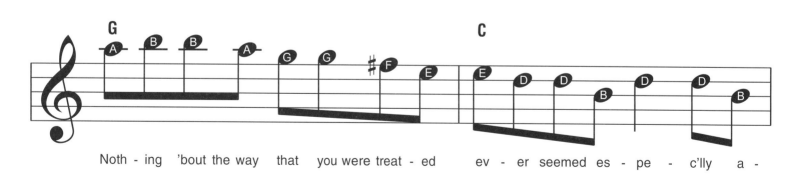

Noth - ing 'bout the way that you were treat - ed ev - er seemed es - pe - c'lly a -

Satellite

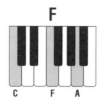
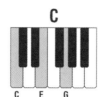
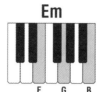

Words and Music by Harry Styles,
Thomas Hull and Tyler Johnson

Sign of the Times

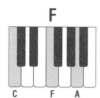

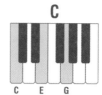

Words and Music by Harry Styles,
Jeff Bhasker, Mitch Rowland, Ryan Nasci,
Alex Salibian and Tyler Johnson

Moderately slow half-time feel

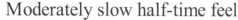

Just stop your cry-ing; it's a sign of the times. ____

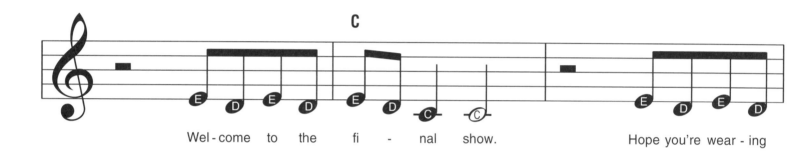

Wel-come to the fi - nal show. Hope you're wear-ing

your ____ best clothes. You can't bribe the door on your way to the

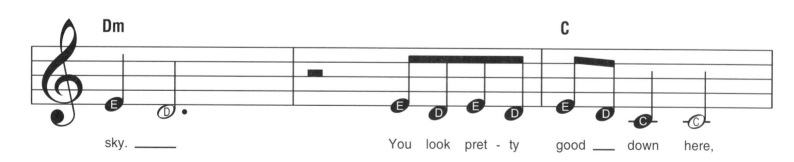

sky. ____ You look pret-ty good ____ down here,

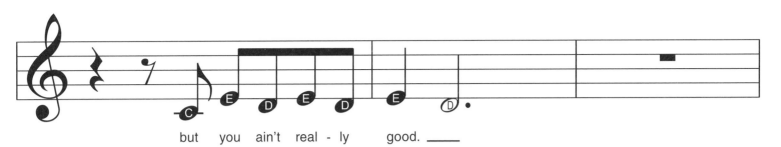

but you ain't real - ly good. _____

We nev - er learn; __ we've been here be - fore.   Why are we al - ways stuck and

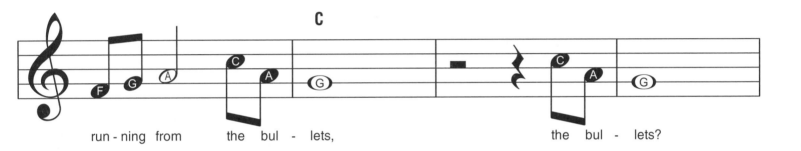

run - ning from   the bul - lets,   the bul - lets?

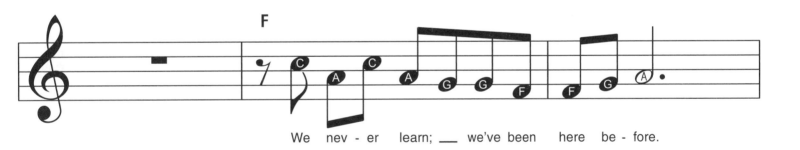

We nev - er learn; __ we've been   here be - fore.

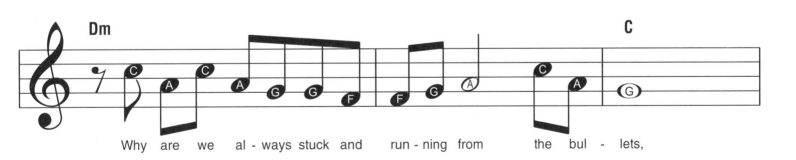

Why are we al - ways stuck and   run - ning from   the bul - lets,

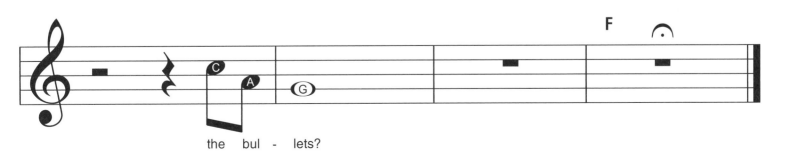

the bul - lets?

Sweet Creature

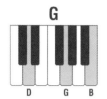
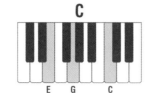
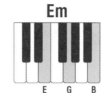
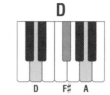
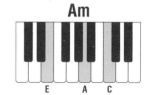

Words and Music by Harry Styles
and Thomas Hull

Moderate Ballad

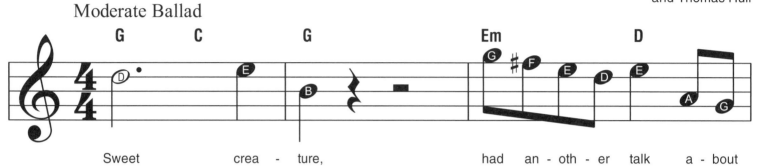

Sweet crea - ture, had an - oth - er talk a - bout

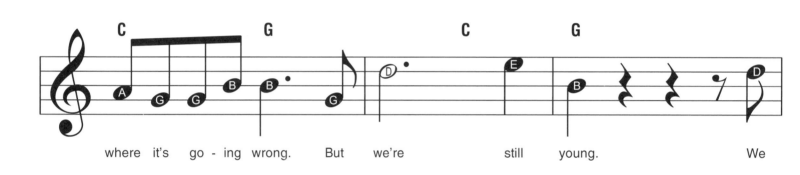

where it's go - ing wrong. But we're still young. We

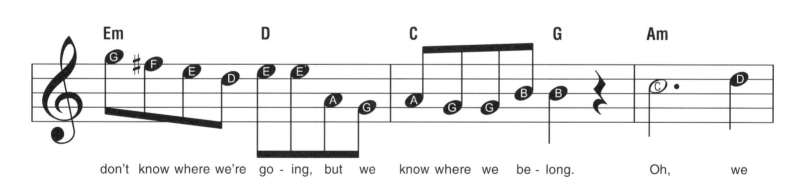

don't know where we're go - ing, but we know where we be - long. Oh, we

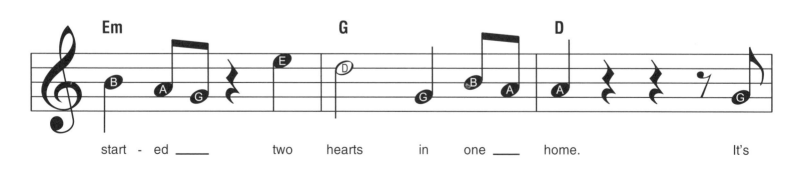

start - ed ____ two hearts in one ____ home. It's

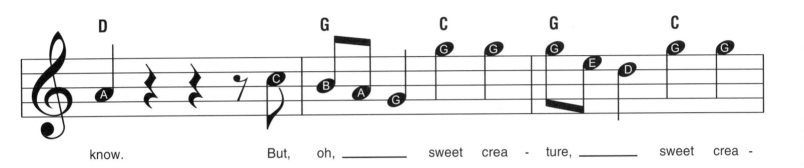

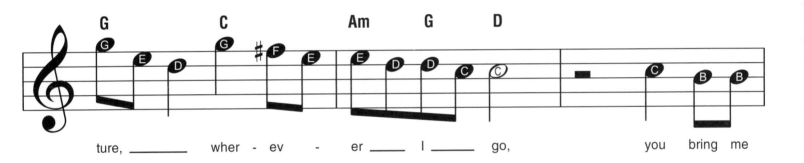

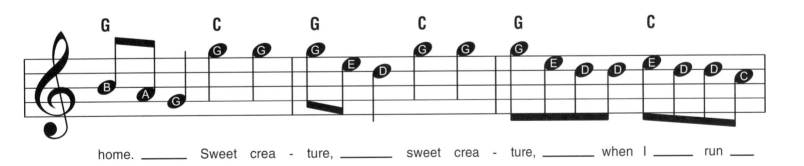

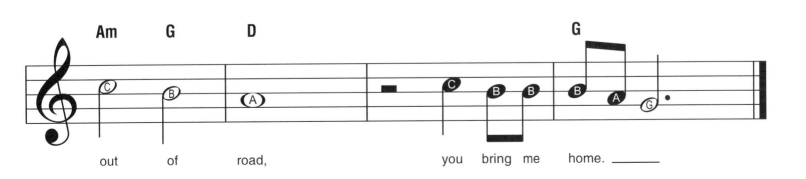

Two Ghosts

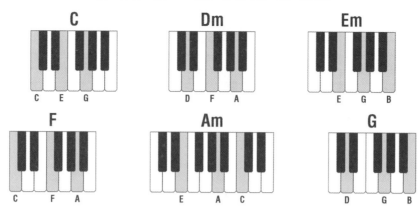

Words and Music by Harry Styles,
Tyler Johnson, John Ryan,
Julian Bunetta and Mitch Rowland

Moderate half-time feel

Same lips red, same eyes blue. Same white shirt, cou - ple

more tat - toos. It's not you and it's not

me. _____ Tastes so sweet,

looks so real. Sounds like some - thing that I used to feel,

29

Watermelon Sugar

 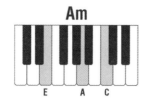 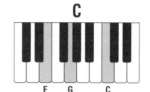 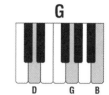

Words and Music by Harry Styles,
Thomas Hull, Mitchell Rowland
and Tyler Johnson

Moderate groove